Breaking

The

Curse

Of

Willie Lynch

THE SCIENCE OF SLAVE PSYCHOLOGY
By Alvin Morrow

RSP **Rising Sun Publications**
11220 W. Florissant Ave. # 206 · Florissant, MO 63033

Breaking

The

Curse

Of

Willie Lynch

THE SCIENCE OF SLAVE PSYCHOLOGY

Breaking The Curse Of Willie Lynch
THE SCIENCE OF SLAVE PSYCHOLOGY
By Alvin Morrow
copyright c 2003 Rising Sun Publications
All Rights Reserved

Cover Artist:
Kevin Bryant INKOSI DESIGN STUDIO 314-361-3984
Editor: Janet M. Brown
First Printing: August 2003
Second Printing: April 2004

Manufactured & Printed in the United States of America
Social Science/Psychology
ISBN 0-9720352-1-4
($9.95)

Published By
Rising Sun Publications
11220 W. Florissant Ave., Florissant, MO 63033
Email: Risinsnpub@aol.com

Phone Number 1(866) 899-0822
WHOLESALE & RETAIL BOOKSELLERS

RSP Rising Sun Publications
11220 W. Florissant Ave. # 206 · Florissant, MO 63033

Breaking The Curse Of Willie Lynch
THE SCIENCE OF SLAVE PSYCHOLOGY
TABLE OF CONTENTS

DEDICATION
PREFACE
FOREWORD

INTRODUCTION

DEDICATION

To the people in America that were kidnapped from Africa, and brought to the shores of the western world as captives in the holds of slave ships. Breaking the Curse Of Willie Lynch is an assignment for all of their descendants. This book is for those who are consciously striving to recover from the psychological wounds brought about by the nature of our unique slave experience. Secondly, this book is for those on the other side of the equation who are honest enough to sincerely look into the major issues of race between Blacks & Whites who co-exist in this ever growing melting pot called America!

PREFACE

During the days of forced involuntary slavery the Africans brought to the shores of North America have been made a part of history in a unique way by being part of the largest kidnapping ever experienced. What makes the Black experience of slavery so unique is not the massive numbers in which we were brought, in the holds of ships captained by European traders, but what was psychologically experienced at the hands of our captors. Based on one sole purpose, we at Rising Sun Publications present to you Breaking The Curse Of Willie Lynch, a man skilled in the art of executing generational psychic chaos, internal conflict, war, and perpetual disunity among the black man & woman once held captive in North America.

Foreword

by Willie Lynch & Alvin Morrow

Gentlemen, I greet you here on the banks of the James River in the year of our Lord One Thousand Seven Hundred and Twelve. First, I shall thank you , the gentlemen of the Colony of Virginia for bringing me here. I am here to help you solve some of your problems with slaves. Your invitation reached me on my modest plantation in the West Indies where I have experimented with some of the newest and oldest methods for control of slaves. Ancient Rome would envy us if my program is implemented. As our boat sailed south on the James River, named for our Illustrious King, whose version of the Bible I cherish. I saw enough to know that your problem is not unique. While Rome used cords of wood as crosses for standing human bodies along it's old highways in great numbers, you are here using the tree and the rope on occasion.

I caught the whiff of a dead slave hanging from a tree a couple of miles back. You are not only losing valuable stock by hangings, you are having uprisings, slaves are running away, your crops are sometimes left in the fields too long for maximum profit, you suffer occasional fires, your animals are killed. Gentlemen, you know what your problems are; I do not need to elaborate. I am here to introduce you to a method of solving them.

Author's comment to reader: what you have just read was the first part of the infamous Willie Lynch speech documented in the year of 1712. This book contains the entire content of Mr. Lynch's instructions & the document (The Making Of A Slave instructions in bold print as points of reference in breaking the curse of slave indoctrination. Enjoy your learning!

Introduction

Breaking The Curse of Willie Lynch is a book written in an attempt to dissect the psychology behind the motive common to most North American Slave Masters. The importance of this subject is timely and necessary for the advancement of the psyche of Black America, and understanding the curse described in The Making Of a Slave, by Willie Lynch himself. It describes to the reader the timely effects of past historical slave conditioning, which lays the foundation for the reader. This new writing explores the realms not only of deception, but the actual tactics of mind control that tie in with the overall Genocide of A Nation, through a form of conditioning intended to have effects on the Black Family for centuries.

Hopefully this analysis will help motivate us to better understand the fabricated fractions beneath the surface of our consciousness, that have been the basis of a damaged family unit in the Black community. My sole intention for this publication is to help us break the repetitive cycle enforced by the psychological division instigated by the words, plans, conditioning, and abuse brought about by use of the methods devised by Willie Lynch and his council.

The central motive in Breaking The Curse Of Willie Lynch is targeted mostly toward the re-positioning of the roles of black men and women, in their relationship based on nature more so than tradition. I will expound on this phenomenon and its chemical damage on a biological level, thus exploring the trauma imposed upon the black slaves from a genetic and hormonal perspective to show the lingering effects of the long-term intentions of the Willie Lynch curse. Deeper investigation on this subject must be completed, if we as a race intend on successfully recovering from the detrimental blows that North American Slavery has had on the minds of an entire segment of the human race.

To the best of my knowledge the concepts of Willie Lynch have never been explained in microscopic detail from beginning to end in book form. I pray that my efforts are skillfully investigated, and studied by black psychologists and scholars of reform. When this process has been activated, then we can truly liberate the black nation's state of mind in the United States of America.

Breaking the Curse of Willie Lynch is written in a manner to lay an historical base in order to stimulate the mind's natural healing process; because the mind and the body are very much alike in essence. These two interacting systems function the same, due to both only process information and food from a standpoint of addition and subtraction. The body does it by discerning healthy nutrients, and the mind discerns truth from falsehood then eliminates the latter.

My goal is to focus on the mental aspect of slavery in it's connection to the biological damage yielded by the implications of Willie Lynch's formula; and at the same time give enough insight to expose his motive as well as the individual character himself. In other words, my purpose for writing this book is to make Willie Lynch as popular as possible, because he should receive proper credit for documenting this often used method of slave making techniques. Mr.Lynch's article should be studied by black religious leaders, scholars, psychologists, and black people in general as the pivotal point for further advancement. This letter contains Mr. Lynch's spirit and mind, and expresses in depth his honest personal motive to be direct, and most bluntly sincere. In truth Black America as a nation still suffers largely due to the implementation of his plan, which at it's, essence revolves around the deprivation of our historical base.

We will cover as many topics in Willie Lynch's Letter as clearly and briefly, with as much detail as possible. Hopefully, this book will shed some light on the minds of black men and women in their present state of thinking, to stimulate understanding, initiate harmony, and develop functional families that will in return strengthen our people. A people unlike any other, that were stolen, brought to the western world, and nearly mentally destroyed beyond repair. Using this book as a foundational pillar, let you the reader, and I begin to unite our understandings in an effort to break the curse of Willie Lynch.

To every person who comes into contact with this book; take the necessary time to apply this information to your present situation. Notice how the instructions in the Willie Lynch letter are still being used in the common work place, religious circles, and the black home. Understanding the division of the black female and the male is essential today, because these two halves are mandatory for the construction of a free spirited, righteous, and civilized society.

The next step of Willie Lynch's instruction is to create a state of mind in the male and female that repetitiously perpetuates un-forgiveness of one another, while at the same time being apologetic and defensive of white authority and it's wrongs.

I pray that this small book is used as a reference guide for our present generation and those that follow. May our study of this great discovery aid us in our quest for peace and harmony, a harmony that has been foreign for many North American black people since the capturing of the first African by the early generations of white slave traders. Many black men and women may ask the question, what is the necessity for writing a book formed by this point of view? Questions of this nature can only be produced based on the reader's assumption that we are completely free. Traditionally we have been made to believe that an actual slave has to be a person physically bound by the shackle, ball, and chain. But time has proven that this is not the case with the Africans who were shackled mentally and trained to voluntarily carry the awesome burden of building the economy of this luxury filled country called America.

How To Read This Book!

The study of this subject matter requires the following instructions. This Book must be read completely from the very beginning to end, and from the end to the beginning in the reverse order in which the chapters were originally arranged. Reading Breaking The Curse Of Willie Lynch in this order is very similar to the process slave makers used to rearrange the black slaves natural orientation of mind. The reason so is to provoke the reader to cover the past and the future order of the effects of such slave conditioning, while staying connected with the present moment. This process allows each individual to break the repetitive cycle that has caused us to sub-consciously pivot from a point of disadvantage. Secondly, keep in mind that words italicized in bold print come directly from the mind, and mouth of professional slave makers during the plantation era.

Chapter One
Slaves In The Making

Let's ask ourselves the question, what makes a person a slave? A slave is a person under the manipulation or physical confines of another brought about by brute force or carefully skilled trickery or deceit. We as a people have already developed a common definition describing the 400 years of forced labor. But many of us have not carefully deciphered the code of the modern slave-making methods of white corporate slaveholders. In a nutshell, a modern slave can easily be defined as person that carries in his or her mind the old ideas, plans, and will of the old traditional slave maker, even though they are no longer physically detained. Normally this discussion would have already have ended, but due to the continued effective nature of Willie Lynch's Letter, we must carry on.

As a foundation, let's examine the words of this letter. In doing so, we will get more in touch with the underlying motive behind Mr. Lynch's psychological motives in developing the method for making the Black man and woman into the type of slave we are about to describe. Somewhere deep down in the mind of the white slave masters, was and still is, a deep fear of the people that they oppress. Beneath that fear is the lack of confidence in their own ability connected to an understanding of the greater ability of the people that they feel must be mastered for purposes of mental security. This state of mind has been internalized and planted more firmly into the heart and soul of black people in the United States, more than any of the other slaves throughout the history and world dominated by white slave makers.

Before going any further, several differences surrounding the trade, and the making of the African into a slave must be made clear. The first point to be made clear is that the actual trade of black slaves did not by itself cause the more potent form of mental damage that blacks suffer from today. Even though families and nations had been physically divided to the point where languages and dialogue had been cut off. From the start, an already developing communication problem had now been amplified and made extremely complicated. Those of us who share the slave experience already see that the present day problems in the black family, are based on the structure that the black family was left with during slavery. This is manifested today in the stress filled tone of communication between many black men and women versus a free flowing dialogue that produces mutual cooperation instead of conflicts between egos. This does not include the exception of the rare cases where black people have re-wedged, and benefited from a stable family unit.

Overall the present issue in the making of a slave over Four Hundred years later, has presented us with the dilemma, that something more serious than the kidnapping, physical murder, and sale of our bodies had to happen to black people here in North America. Notice that in any discipline where one may strive to obtain the level of mastery, the objective in mastering something difficult is that the subject has to become easy to master. Making overcoming the diffi- culty in the control factor of your subject, is a sign that you have successfully mastered the subject. During the time in history when black bodies were clothed in chains, the slave master obviously saw a flaw in his tactics of control when enforcing his barbaric practices of torture, fear, beating, and murder by example to obtain control when dealing with his Negro slaves. The problem described in this book lies more along the lines of the slave master's desire to implement a more evolved type of control over his human live- stock.

Today most blacks are still a segregated group living under America's failing economy, and are short of the basic desired goal of freedom which includes control of our time, destiny, and money. We will look at Willie Lynch's program from the position of a long range plan of economic development, and profitable security. How could you enslave, rape, mistreat, and even kill the family members of those under your authority; and at the same time secure the making of a slave and make monetary profits? What must be done to the mind of a people who have gone through such conditioning, and still carry on their daily service to the people who have perpetrated this atrocity nearly a century and a half after they have been so called freed?

The Caucasian slave masters understood the depths of their own psyche in relation to the true dif- ferences between the phrases "slave maker", and "slave master". The first three hundred years of

American enslavement of the African dealt with the physical captivity, export, and the trade of black bodies. But there is a second phase to this story, that incorporates the two different understandings stated. Black people as a whole must not only define things for our selves, to color and set the tone of our own picture (reality), but we must understand in detail the definitions of those who continue in their attempt to further control our future. The slave maker can be defined as a person who uses the barbaric tactics of torture, fear, beating, and murder by example alone, to obtain control. Secondly, a slave master is a person who has studied the spirit, soul, and psychology on a subject in order to master the internal operating principles that actually makes the person tick.

Historically, a title had not up until recently been given to this system, nor had an individual been credited with the development and packaging of such a productive system until the discovery of Willie Lynch's Letter. Lynch and company somehow were able to conceptualize the very essence of slave making methods. The amazement of the matter is that after reading the letter two hundred and ninety years later, the spiritual drugs of division documented in the archives of this speech have held true exactly as Mr. Lynch stated. (The minimum test of time, in which this method if used would control the minds of the Negro Slave for at least 300 years.)

The second phase of the curse of Willie Lynch included the strong prediction that the utilization of his method would ensure the control of the Negro state of mind for at least an entire melinimum (thousand) years. My question to challenge the thoughts of the reader is: can we afford another generation of ours to continue the slave master/slave relationship? Well, what must be done and studied to prevent the continued tradition of this relationship? Because whether we realize it or not, white America no longer has the need for a co-dependent relationship with the once shackled slave. To make matters worse, the American economy after the September 11th bombing can no longer support the weight of carrying the responsibility of a mastered slave.

Chapter Two
Black Animalization

What we do with horses is that we break them from one form of life to another; that is we reduce them from the natural state in nature; whereas nature provides them with the natural capacity to take care of their needs and the needs of their offspring, we break that natural string of independence from them and their by create a dependency state so that we may be able to get from them useful production for our business and pleasure.

The wounds acquired from the slave experience over time have inflicted enough physical, social, and economic damage to prove that blacks as a people have been animalized. Before going any further, let's review the definition of animal as described in Webster's Dictionary: (1.any such organism other than a human being: 2.a brutish, debased, or inhuman person.) Here we will expound on the second description stating that an animal is inhuman, or debased. When something or someone has been debased they become disconnected from their foundation. In the process they are detached from the very core of their being that gives them value. That is the case of the Negro slave. The very culture, norms, and values that allowed us to uplift and civilize our citizens according to our own standard.

What makes man and woman civilized? What makes us un-civilized? A people are considered civilized when they act in accordance to their understanding of the knowledge of the nature of themselves. In the reverse, a people become un-civilized when they become subject and governed by the lower negative element of their nature, which in most cases is due to the absence of an inherent relative self knowledge connecting them to mother nature, that some call the universe or God. In the process of making a slave, the African was eventually stripped of any remaining background that would allow the black masses to connect with their natural divinity, or even yet claim any kinship to being made in the image and likeness of God.

Wise people throughout the ages have taught us to know thyself. But in the life of the overwhelming majority of Negro slaves confined to the American plantation, there was never provided the opportunity under safe conditions that would enable the Negro to ever publicly regain his humanity. In most cases the stronger or more educated Negro was killed outright in front of the rest of the slaves as an example of what happens to a Nigger boy slave, when he decides to become a human. This example was then, and is presently used as a system of checks and balances in order to mentally produce fear in the Negro thus hindering an entire race of people from achieving true liberation.

Making man exist in the state of an animal is a twofold process. First, there is the destruction of decent morals, which include the perversion of the people's traditional native religious practices, and governing social norms. These laws, rules, and regulations serve as guidelines, or a people's internal fortress to protect the society and its citizens from foreign disruption, and disorder. As during the years of physical bondage, the bulk of the black community today is suffering internally because of the debasement of our human foundation. That foundation consisted of a high level of moral ethical conduct supported by belief in the laws of nature.

Secondly, the dehumanization of the African happened during the entire process of kidnapping, sale, and forced enslavement. This included the housing of the masses of slaves in hay filled barns with the beasts of the field. A process that included the installation of gold or silver caps on the front teeth of the black slave for the purpose of identification, that many of us today wear for decoration. In most cases this was the treatment given to the house Negroes, but most wore the masters mark burned by the branding iron heated with burning coals. This is one of the early stages of dehumanization suffered by the Negro slave. And like then, today many of us wear the symbols of the legacy of our oppressors on our black bodies.

This second phase deals with the spiritual perversion of a people based on training the Black African under a western psychologically domesticated system of indoctrination. This starts the very moment when a people are stripped of the personal duties and responsibilities of doing for themselves under a system organized and constructed by their own peers. The Willie Lynch method explained this as the creation of a state of dependency. In modern terms a welfare state, and any black male or female that does anything other than the norm could easily be classified as an enemy of the state. We as black people should be aware that the moment we begin to depend on someone else to do for us (what with unity we can do for ourselves), we have given them power over our lives. This automatically gives the old slave master, and his offspring the upper hand.

As a nation, blacks continued to suffer economically during the era of the Freedman's Bureau. In our ignorance to do something for ourselves, we were forced to turn right back around and offer black labor to the former slave masters in the form of sharecropping.

Look very carefully at the name of the committee organized to conceptualize, and define what freedom would be to the Negro slave, after being released from their state of physical captivity. The word Freed in the term Freedman's Bureau implies that we were released by the permission of another power, and we had no responsibility in the planning of our own liberation. Proof is in the underlying root meaning of Freed man. We as a people well never get true respect equal to the level of other nations, because we had nothing to do with our own freedom. Therefore One Hundred and Thirty-seven years later, we still do not enjoy, nor do we benefit from the fruits of our labor as a whole like people from other cultures that have recently crossed over the borders of North America.

Chapter Three
Understanding Divisions

In my bag here, I have a fullproof method for controlling your black slaves. I guarantee every one of you that if installed correctly, it will control the slaves for at least Three hundred years. My method is simple. Any member of your family or your overseer can use it.

I have outlined a number of differences among the slaves, and I take these differences and make them bigger. I use fear, distrust, and envy for control purposes. These methods have worked on my modest plantation in the West Indies and it will work through out the South. Take this simple little list of differences, and think about them. On top of my list is "Age" but it is there only because it starts with an "A"; the second is "Color" or shade, there is intelligence, size, sex, size of plantations, status on plantation, attitude of owners, whether the slaves live in the valley, on the hill, East, West, North, South, have fine hair, course hair, or is tall or short. Now that you have a list of differences, I shall give you an outline of action- but before that I shall assure you that distrust is stronger than trust, and envy is stronger than adulation, respect or admiration.

The Black slave after receiving this indoctrination shall carry on and will become self re-fueling and self generating for hundreds of years, maybe thousands.

Don't forget you must pitch the old Black male vs the young Black male, and the young Black male against the old Black male. You must use the dark skin slaves vs the light skin slaves and the light skin slaves vs the dark skin slaves. You must use the female vs the male, and the male vs the female. You must also have your white servants and overseers distrust all Blacks, but it is necessary that your slaves trust and depend on us. They must love, respect and trust only us.

Although, this instructional speech was delivered by Willie Lynch on the banks of the James River in the year of 1712. These same tactics are still being applied in the workplace, and on the black family in the year 2003 and beyond. Before going any further, at this point we must come to the agreement that at the foundation of the slave makers thinking was and still is, the belief that the Negro male and female must remain divided and ignorant, in order that his system may function according to his plans, uninterrupted in an orderly fashion.

While we are all involved in the process of breaking the curse of Willie Lynch, we must be sure not to add fuel to the fire that has broken down an entire nation of people. This fuel consists of the constant outside instigation, and magnification of our differences. In the process of dividing the black male and the female, the objective of control became easier due to the fact that the slave makers only have a half of a people to manage. This is the reason for the manipulation of differences. Because once you split a peoples commonly shared ideal, you can divide the individuals even further by injecting a foreign concept as a solution once they have been split apart.

A common example in the lives of black people, takes place in domestic disputes mediated by so called white authorities, peace-keepers or social workers. We invite them into our homes to solve the very problems their fore-parents created. These are the descendants of Willie Lynch's people, that created and instigated the artificial problems that we constantly wrestle with one another over. Often, in the black community, money problems take center stage in the drama, more so when there is a surplus than when there is a shortage. When there is a shortage the stress is on what type of material benefits can we acquire with a certain level of income. On the other hand when there is a surplus, the argument between the man and the woman, is over the management of the finances. Then comes the systematic mediators instigating the drama played out in the domestic courts, and there you have it: another black family becoming more consumed by Willie Lynch's curse.

Legal division mainly falls under the category of courts, marriages, and divorces, that are certified by mainstream white authority. This act alone gives another man the control to decide the fate of black unity. And in doing so we as black men and women re-enforce the belief in the minds of the so called white authorities that we aren't man and woman enough to decide, plan, and solve our problems aside from his input, which is only mere deceit. Even before the documenting of these divisive methods so widely accredited to Willie Lynch, the method of divide and conquer has been an age old policy systematized by White Nations when dealing with Nations of color.

Most of the situations that fall under this category are usually decided over by an authority appointed mediator who tricks the black man and woman by not talking to both of them at the same time. They aid in the separating of the black man and woman first of all by providing an instant easy solution to their problems. Of course their answer to their problems with black men and women, is to encourage us to dissolve our union. Just quit, don't even try uniting, because this is not what we planned for you niggers to do. This is the mind of the modern maintainers of the plantation. Today the plantation represents, the artificial conflict of interest between black men and woman.

What needs to be done in the relationships of black men and women is that we need to develop, and define a cultural agenda. An agenda systematically structured to over run any of our personal desires that serve, and benefit the opposition, thereby dissolving those goals that breed envy, instigate division, and the spiritual lynching of black families. We have, through four decades of conditioning been made to believe and practice a foreign peoples dictated life style. This Euro-centric practice of individual independence of man and woman makes it look like blacks are directly the sole cause of the destruction of their own family structure.

Chapter Four
The Psycho Alteration Of The Bio-Chemical

Following are a few paragraphs from the document written by Willie Lynch and furthermore introduced and practiced by millions of white slave masters all over the country. This part is a reference point to the antidote that Lynch and his following feared, concerning the future of American slave economics.

Our experts warned us about the possibility of this phenomenon occurring, for they say the mind has a strong drive to correct and re-correct itself over a period of time, if it can touch substantial original historical base; and they advised us that the best way to deal with the phenomenon is to shave off the brute's mental history and create a multiplicity of phenomena of illusion that each illusion will twirl in it's own orbit, something similar to floating balls in a vacuum. This creation of a multiplicity of phenomena of illusions entails the principles of cross-breeding the nigger and the horse as we stated above, the purpose of which is to create a diversified division of labor thereby creating different levels of labor and different values of illusions at each connecting level of labor, the results of which is the severance of the points of original beginnings for each sphere of illusion.

Before going any further into the traumatic after effects of Willie Lynch and his equals, let us understand that every thought the human mind has, immediately produces a chemical equal in response to that particular thought. Based on the intensity level of the event or given set of circumstances, the individual or group of people under such conditions will produce a common chemical bond synonymous with those events. In the case of the black man and woman under the program of such skillful slave makers, the black slaves were intentionally frozen in a fixed state of terror, ignorance, and self hatred toward their self and kind.

The three previous chapters described the base conditioning, which are the remaining results. Brought about by the bio-chemical altering of black consciousness during the traumatic process of breaking the black slave. Never before on the record of time or on the record of any nation's history has there been such a scientifically crafted and executed method of mind control. What makes this type of mind control so long lasting and unique? The success of Mr. Lynch's doctrine is not merely based on the instigation, exaggeration, and magnification of economic, physical characteristics, and sexual gender differences, but also the effects brought about based on the bio-chemical, or hormonal effects produced and recorded in the physical anatomy of the black man and woman through four centuries of intentional shocking of the neurological system. We must realize that once a certain thought is repeated in the mind, there is left in the chemistry of the individual a recorded imprint, that actually blends into and bonds with the genetic structure of the human cell.

Now that we have laid down some of the basic fundamentals for understanding why Willie Lynch's impact has had such long-term effects on the black man and woman, let us expand our understanding of the intensity of this wisely executed form of indoctrination. Let us remember, that we are not focusing in on the physical capture, rape, and bondage of the black body, though this does lay the foundation for the Euro-Slave masters method of bio-chemical and mental destruction.

Our purpose for discussing this subject matter is solely to give you a clear description of the detailed damage on a microscopic level, and to show why we as black men and women have not been able to put a complete end to the widespread madness of internal conflict and division. Beneath the surface of the sub-conscious mind of the African brought to the Northern part of America, is an indoctrination of divisions firmly planted in the core of our sub-conscious mind that has chemically penetrated the black genetic structure. The depth of the Willie Lynch letter reaches far beyond basic mind control, it is a scientifically detailed psychology that can only be reversed and broken based on one method. That method is effective only if the Four Hundred year old Bio-chemical method is severed on a cellular level.

During the physical slave process, why did the slave master use tactics of fear, envy, jealously, and distrust while he had already maintained physical control of his captured human stock? Why were the previous elements of social control necessary after the black man and woman were apparently held in check, and in the grip of the chain and shackle?

Remember earlier when we mentioned that there was only one method to completely break the curse of Willie Lynch? Well, we must also consider that Mr. Lynch and his comrades understood that there was only one proper method in the making of a slave, and that is the artificial fabrication of consciousness. That could only take place when the previous database in the human mind could be deleted permanently, totally destroyed, and trashed forever. That data being the history of black people's past material accomplishments combined with black people's personal understanding of their own disciplines. These are classified as the human developmental sciences, which are the basis for a complete knowledge of self.

According to Mr. Lynch and company there was one, and only one antidote that would undo this bio-chemical perversion. "Authors Comment" **Being a Professional Wholistic Health Care Nutritionist I found it necessary to explain the effects of four hundred years of terror, destruction, and instigated division of differences from a bio-chemical basis of understanding. My reason for this approach is simple, so that the masses of our people are clear in that we understand the long term Bio-chemical effects of what we have been brought through as an entire race, or nation of people.**

"Authors comment." The fact that a breeding process was considered in conjunction with the shaving off of the mental history proves that the slave master and their wise council had a perfect understanding of the bio-chemical effects on the black slave during bondage. Also their long-term future results, that are still affecting the black man and woman bio-logically today. Note that a people's geographic and physical history, are only taught to the mass population. Eurocentric historians do not make the mistake in teaching the pure mental history in their curriculum, and public text, because to do so would now be classified in a class called social sciences. Social sciences communicate to students the cultural norms, which include the religion, spiritual disciplines, morals, family values, and traditions. By getting the black masses into an in-depth study of these sciences, along with proper diet will automatically trigger the proper chemical effect, from the brain through the central nervous system taping into and reversing the condition of a contaminated cell structure. Since our subject involves the undoing of the socio-spiritual knot that has bound the black man and woman, and at the same time divided the black family. We need to begin with the initiation methods of the conditioning that we as a people received early on in the slave making process.

First, the shaving off the mental history of an entire nation of people, has very little or nearly nothing to do with the past historical, geographical, or physical accomplishments of an ethnic group. In Breaking The Curse Of Willie Lynch, this point must be made clear because as black people in this late day in time now have abundant access to our genetic, and physical past. Well we are still scattered and fragmented when it comes to being effectively organized and pro-actively productive for the benefit of the whole.

The mental history includes, and is defined as follows: every tool used in the form of self development from religion to Metaphysics, Meditation, and spiritual traditions. Since we are dealing with the destruction of the bio-chemistry of the black man and woman, let's connect the mental history with the physical body so we may wholistically cover this topic. In reversing the effects of a bio-chemical slavery, we must realize that the Black African brought to the Northern part of America, had lost the historical aspects of our physical sciences such as ancient methods of physical fitness, massage, reflexology, breathing techniques, and the original disciplines of the martial arts which are all exceptional tools of self discipline, development, growth and mastery. From both a biological and chemical level, we must understand that there is a connection with these two spheres within the human mechanism. The connection or, in the case dealing with Willie Lynch's techniques, the disconnection includes the dis-functionalization of the inner accessible sphere of the black human mechanism, which is the physical transmitter of waves, ideas, hormones and chemicals. That intermediate sphere is the physical brain.

To make the proper alterations in order to re-customize the psychological state of the black mind black, educators, psychologist, scientist, and doctors of wholistic medicine must first access the proper tools for undertaking the task at hand. Second, in breaking the curse of Willie Lynch, the black masses must come to grips with the reality that we have been thinking about ourselves as black people from the basis and format of an adversary, foreign in spirit, mind, body, and in nature.

Expounding on the warning that the slave making letter, which in it's contents gave credibility to some of the possible interloping negatives documented surrounding the "Mental History" of the black, once-physical slave. Which is relative to the recorded history of the black man and woman brought into slavery upon the shores of North America, is the overwhelming shock to the natural conscious mind brought about by such an energy draining loss of the historical mind's data base.

What was the psychological basis for the Euro-centered psychologist fearing the unraveling of their indoctrination of the black slave? This fear was and is still based upon black people affected by this doctrine gaining back a substantial original historical base, which is due to the fact that they re-obtained the knowledge of self. Their intuitive memory and natural faculties would be re-activated, and all of the genetic potential would become fully accessible.

Let us review Mr.Willie Lynch's slave psychologist definition of the word phenomenon. According to their definition based on our condition, phenomenon means something rare, an occurrence beyond ordinary observation and inspires awe and wonder. *Based on a previous quote by Senator Henry Berry in 1832 while addressing the Virginia House Of Delegates "we have extinguished every avenue by which light could enter into the mind of the black slave. If we could extinguish their capacity to see the light, our work would be complete. They would then be on a level with the beasts of the field; and we would be safe. I am not certain that we would not do it, if we could find out the process; and that on the plea of necessity!"* Well according to the slave masters in the past, and the present generation of oppressors, what has been, and is occurring in this country concerning black men and women whose minds have been activated based on an exposure to literature and scholarship of our great historical heritage can be classified as a phenomenon.

Inclusive of the historical data base of every culture, are the medical healing arts, sciences, and health traditions. What is more distinct to one's culture than the foods that its constituents depend upon for daily sustenance? Nothing, food is the substance of life made from the same earth elements comprising human life. These are especially important in the function of the mind, unlocking dormant mental, physical, and even spiritual potential.

Reflecting upon the hygiene and dietary circumstances on the plantation scene, as well as the present moment for many blacks as a collective, we must be mindful of the condition of the black man and woman's health. The present diet that nearly eighty percent of black people consume is comprised of the same foods we were forced to eat during the four centuries of forced servitude to white plantation slave owners. Very little has changed since those days except that physical exercise has become a voluntary activity in the daily life of our people. Today, outside of college and professional sports, required physical educational classes most of us due to the lack of health awareness begin to take the bodily journey down hill.

Comprising a list of all of the foods that were made a part of the black slaves diet upon being introduced to new life on the plantation. Foods like Pinto Beans, Lima Beans and Black Eyed Peas that are overloaded with acid and destructive to the digestive system. Other basics are the leafy greens, like mustard, turnips, and collard greens which the black man and woman of today consume on a regular basis. The consumption of leafy green foods that are, highly concentrated in vitamin K, which is the active ingredient responsible for the production of blood clots. Excessive vitamin K is the silent enemy to the circulatory system due to the fact that it thickens the blood, putting a strain on the veins, and arteries. Not to mention that excessive vitamin K in the blood is in a large measure responsible for so many of the strokes, and high blood pressure that black people suffer from. These are some of the foods that we are accustomed to calling soul food, which in truth demote the body's balance.

On the other side of the table, there are those of us who are willing to spend that extra dollar for a tasty meal, such as fresh water or sea foods, such as shrimps, clams, and crabs, which are scavengers. Meaning they consume the caucus, and defecation of other animals for their survival. **Knowledge of Health,** is just as important in Breaking The Curse Of Willie Lynch as understanding the rudiments of his slave making process. The following are some basic nutritional tips for enhancing food through supplements. First, and most common is the stress factor due to the circumstances of black men and women's experience and present existence. Black people in America carry more stress, and fat than the average person. We also carry more blood sugar imbalances and are dying from diabetes faster and more frequently than the average citizen in this country. Physical ailments of this nature are unnatural, and are actually the symptoms reflecting damage penetrating deep to the black mind. To ease some of the basic dis-ease contained in the blood, muscular, and even the nerve cells, you should consume at least 100 milligrams of a vitamin B complex daily. Stay away from all white foods except cauliflower, onions, & garlic; no consumption of white sugar, potatoes, white rice, and white flour. These foods convert to starch, to sugar creating diabetic conditions. Low vitamin B counts increase the chance for this condition, which stems from the traditional plantation diet. Vitamin B's are responsible for the assimilation of blood glucose levels, which has a lot to do with fighting stress and the metabolizing of extra fat in the body.

The B complex vitamins are essential to the proper nervous system function. They have allot to do with the children in their learning process, especially children diagnosed with attention deficit disorder. Children diagnosed with this condition are as normal as any other child in their learning ability, except their development is thwarted due to a heavy vitamin B deficiency. Adults who consume coffee on a daily basis also suffer from nervous tension, and weak bones because caffeine robs the body of vitamin B's and Calcium. Other information on health can be obtained elsewhere, but we had to stress its importance because it is fifty percent of the equation when habiliating, and elevating the conscious level of the people.

Chapter Five
Breaking Competitive Barriers

Gaining a complete understanding of how the captured African was made a slave can only be done based on understanding divisions, and by breaking all competitive barriers. To the masters of slaves these barriers fabricated between the enslaved serve as the foundation for easy long term control. In brief, we will examine in detail the foundational content of Willie Lynch's doctrine, and display the psychological parallel from the past to the present. This parallel shows us that Mr. Lynch was not only confident but correct in his prophesied calculations concerning his control method's ability to stand the test of time, if not interrupted.

Since we are in a time where freedom of the mind and spirit are known essentials to the survival of the body, we as ex-physical slaves must take into consideration the fact that freedom of our minds is essential for unity and overall survival. In this process of breaking the curse of Willie Lynch, we have to expose ourselves to a process that has taken root on our own thought process that until recently, we ourselves as a collective have not been aware of.

At this point shall we proceed with clarifying the actual motive of Mr. Willie Lynch's in-doctrination of the African mind given to us in his very own words quoted in document as follows.

We breed two nigger males with two nigger females. Then we take the nigger males from them and keep them moving and working. Say the one nigger female bears a nigger female and the other bears a nigger male. Both nigger females, being without the influence of the nigger image, frozen with an independent psychology, will raise their offspring into reverse positions one with the female offspring will teach her to be life herself, independent and negotiable (we negotiate with her, through her, by her and negotiate her at will). The one with the nigger male offspring, she being frozen with a subconscious fear for his life, will raise him to be mentally dependent and weak, but physically strong-- in other words, body over mind. Now in a few years when these two off springs become fertile for early reproduction, we will mate and breed them and continue the cycle. That is good, sound, and long range comprehensive planning.

What we see occurring between black males and females in relationships is a constant power struggle until the dominance of one individual over another is finally decided. In seventy five percent of the cases the black man and woman usually end up cutting ties or dissolving the marriage. We have failed to realize that the Euro-gentile slave master mastered the craft of manipulating the feminine and masculine natures, and benefited from the chaos produced as an end result. In detail, the chaos is produced when the natural internal order of the people's masculine and feminine energies are twisted. In other words when the natural leader's senses are dulled to the point where self guidance is no longer present; and he begins to follow the follower - organization or family soon deteriorates. These tactics were initiated, made public and standardized in 1712 by Willie Lynch, and millions of other slave masters. And ultimately the end result of their vision was reinforced, by a divide and conquer technique of black men and women in the name of women's liberation.

Women's liberation for black females is one of the illusions designed to twirl a string of confusion in the subconscious of black females who are dissatisfied with black male female relations. The Euro-gentile women's rights movement was and is foremost a movement to deal with problems between white men and women, but some how some black women have been drawn into another woman's struggle. The liberation movement of the white female stems from her own inferiorization, and dissatisfaction of white male disloyalty to her on the plantation, which is where her jealousy of the black woman takes it's root. When black women are invited or recruited into these sodomus organizations they are not aware that this is a manifestation of the Euro-gentile white female's psychological vengeance, by leading her into competition with her black male. Throughout our ancient African history there has never been a free woman with out a free man, and vice versa.

To recover from such a forged wall of mental blocks and divisions, black men and women must understand that with time there is evolution of method. We should also know that black male economic incarceration and black female liberation is the reflection of the evolution of slave methodology. On top of being divided by age, color, size, level of education, and sex are the new additions supplied by time. These artificial additives used to continue the break up between the black male and the female are income, class, public status, political party, and most damaging to black people is religious denomination.

Very briefly let us examine the language used to describe **de-nomi-nation**. The **"de"** means to separate, **"nomi"** comes from the Latin word **"nominare"** which means to name. **"Nation"** speaks for it all in reference to black people being a separated nation within ourselves. As we can see, by studying the root languages that make up the English language we are brought closer to the underlying motive of those that oppress through the tactic of divide and conquer. The word nation in its root stems from the latin word **"natalis"** pertains to ones birth in connection to their nature.

Therefore, to denominate means to divide a people from themselves, or bring them down from their original nature. This separation from our original nature has carried over in the case of Willie Lynch's doctrine when put into application to black male/female relationships, and has dramatically affected black people in this section of North America in general.

Chapter Six
Fixing Marriages Breaking Old Social Cycles

In order to gain a complete understanding of the long term effects of Willie Lynch's instructions as they apply to black men and women we will start in the present moment, then travel back in time. In doing so we can pinpoint the very seed idea harvested and planted into the mind of the African man and woman during the plantation years. Very little in the arena of western sociology, and human psychology has been able to accurately dispel or correct the cycle of the fragmented black family. This cycle spins on a mass scale in today's modern black community, and parallels the same system of that in physical slavery. It only differs in that most of its victims are consciously unaware of the material differences allocated by time and circumstance.

For these reasons we must dissect the remnants of the black family, and in doing so we have to deal with the most important factors in any relationship. These factors involving family life include, purpose, function, and importance surrounding present survival. Our examination for reversing the past results must be done exactly as Willie Lynch and company did. They gave their careful attention to stimulating natural chaos, which was rooted in perverting the natural positions of the roles of the male and the female. Mr. Lynch's program of modern day destruction of the black family is a result of psychic-chaos based on the reversal and manipulation of the nature of the male & female.

Today there is no difference in the level of social climate in the black community when compared to the condition of the black man and woman on the plantation. On the plantation scene blacks produced for the slave master a new generation of labor during our younger years, and were the forcibly separated based on the dis-empowering of the black male. The black male was mostly used as a breeding stud to the point where natural responsibility input was viewed as not needed, due to the fact her children had been taken and turned over to the present authorities as a result of an absent, dis-empowered, or un-productive black male. Today in America the same circumstances exist, but the only difference is that the setting is more decorated due to modern transportation, the range of motion for the black slave is more broad.

In a sense what has happened to the very core of the black family unit based on the un-natural reversing of gender is compared to nature turning in on itself and convulsing in a backward chaotic momentum. Using the above statements as a basis for fixing marriages and breaking the old social economic pattern of multiply and divide, which is supported by the Willie Lynch factor of divide and conquer. It seems that in this modern era of technical and moral genocide the greater our numbers as a collective black mass, the weaker we become, because our multiplication only creates more confusion due to the inherited methods of slaveries ingrained automated system of division.

Presently these reversed behavioral patterns are reflected in today's modern black male/female relationships and are reinforced by a social economic structure that is based on a government civil rights policy made legal in the 1960s. This refers to the laws surrounding the hiring of black and women classified as minorities. Hiring a black female, economically eliminates or dis-empowers the black male, by meeting two quotas while employing one person. A policy very similar to the one set up by the Pharaoh in the book of Exodus during the days of Moses, when the policy was to kill all of the male children of that particular generation and spare the female. Well what is the difference between those systems of Affirmative Action that devalued the male economically to the extent that he was made dysfunctional and deemed a liability in the eyes of the female companion of his own race?

By acknowledging the level of damage done to the black psyche connected to the role-altering divisive tactics due to centuries of Willie Lynch's indoctrination, we can then embark upon the path of habilitation and reconciliation in today's black male/female relationships. As a collective, black men and women must also come to intelligent agreement that our natural pattern of motion has been thrown out of orbit, which is reflected in chaotic relationships void of divine natural order. In one sense of the word we have become unconsciously lawless in terms of constructive relationships and family structure. This unnatural occurrence cannot be found taking place among any of the people of color in connection to the native lands from which the black man and woman of North

America stem from. If this circumstance has historically been the case, we black people, the children of
slaves must conclude that we are the manifested bi-
product of Willie Lynch and company's ultimate
intention.

During the early days of traditional physical
slavery the generational male/female cycle rotated
like traffic in a revolving door. Black men and women
bred children without courtship, then were often separated on the plantation or sold to other plantations.
The children were in a sense wards of the state,
because of social and economic breakdown and frag-
mentation of their parents. When the black male was
destroyed and dis-empowered even as many still are
today, millions of black women were left as widows
and their children left out in the wilderness as
orphans. This is a traditional cycle that in the present
moment continues to spin out of natural orbit without
little effort from the slave master's offspring, who subtly steer, guide, and control the very people who are
still the core behind the success of this great economy.

Four hundred and forty-six years later the old
mind of black slave and white master have not yet
been altered. We often wonder why they haven't
based on the following quote by Willie Lynch, ask
yourself the question: Why was the reversal of the
roles between the black male and fe- male such a necessary ingredient in gaining total control over the
black man and woman? So much to the extent, that
this perverted altering of the natural roles between the
man and woman would insure the white slave master
future control for many more generations to come.

The following statement contains the living thoughts practiced by slave masters taken from the making of a slave document.

Understanding is the best thing. Therefore, we shall go deeper into this area of the subject matter concerning what we have produced here in this breaking process of the female nigger. We have reversed the relationships. In her natural uncivilized state she would have a strong dependency on the uncivilized nigger male, and she would have a limited protective tendency toward her independent male offspring and would raise the female offspring to be dependent like her. Nature had provided for this type of balance. We reversed nature by burning and pulling one civilized nigger apart and bull whipping the other to the point of death--all in her presence. By her being left alone, unprotected, with the male image destroyed, the ordeal caused her to move from her psychological dependent state to a frozen independent state. In this frozen psychological state of independence she will raise her male and female offspring in reversed roles. For fear of the young male's life, she will psychologically train him to be mentally weak and dependent but physically strong.

Because she has become psychologically independent, she will train her female offspring psychologically independent. What have you got? You've got the nigger woman out front and the man behind and scared. This is a perfect situation for sound sleep and economics.

Chapter Seven
Willies Fear:
The Phenomenon
Of
True History

For the slave masters to justify an act of mental genocide, they realized then and now that the first casualty of a war must be the truth. This is what is referred to as shaving off the brute's mental history. The phenomena that Mr. Lynch and other slave masters feared, was the so called nigger savages psychological reaction upon the moment of receiving a true historical revelation about themselves. This fear represents to the slave master a loss of control, major lifestyle adjustments, and the actual loss of an entire civilization that was based on superficial speculations that gave them the mental edge over the societies that make up the human population.

Over the last century we have witnessed this fear manifested in the Euro-centric man's aggression to be the center of power through dishonest media, acts of economic sanctions, and acts of physical violence on people of color. What do the so-called most powerful people on the earth fear, and have they become enslaved to the guilt produced by the lies, mistreatment, and control tactics that were used in making the African a mental slave? Since we are dissecting the powerful nature of truth, let us understand that truth is a two-edged sword that cuts the presented as well as the presenter. Therefore, in breaking the curse of Willie Lynch the two spheres of thinking that allow this mind to exist must both face the reality of truth.

Covering the sphere of mind possessed by the black man and woman of North America, there is the tremendous task of analyzing the damaged psyche that under normal circumstances would be supported by a people's mental history. After centuries of physical bondage, black people in America were left with a voided mental history as a basis to start the process of healing. In attempting to educate the black man and woman of North America, the Euro-centric educators in most instances have deliberately calculated a fragment of the Africans history that covered our experience in this country and defined those selected events as a basis of self knowledge for black students.

The educational curriculum that is being used in the United States, does not cater to the basic needs of black students in the area of reform from slaveries psychological damage. This is more noticeable in the area of unified people development. Unified people development is a concept used in the educational systems throughout the more independent nations, even though the concept may be worded differently. This concept can be defined as a system of teaching the students of a particular people to learn and apply their teachers instructions for the betterment of their own people first; as long as they do not harm other groups of people in the progressive process.

On the other side of the truth is the fear in the psyche of many Euro-ethnic students who have been fed a plate of lies about their black student peers as well as about their own history in the world, not only in the area of human accomplishment but in the arena of civil social treatment of human beings other than themselves. This fear of truth levels the playing field in the mind of black and white students, though benefiting the totally misinformed black student greatly. But not to the extent of Black children educated and taught in a social environment owned and operated by a staff specializing in black child development. Since we as black people have a specific and unusual set of issues at hand, let us focus more on our half of breaking the curse of Willie Lynch's effects on the black mind. As seen by black scholars, historians, and educators, we soon became able to gauge the level of our damage not only by our lack of unity, reform, and productivity, but also based on the fearful response to black people's possible unity and self empowerment by those who had enslaved African people.

Fear is defined as a psychologically emotional reaction to the threat of pain, harm, and loss of what is deemed as   mentally or physically essential to a healthy life. In a more modern explanation of the definition of fear, is the undermining of common comfort by an outside power or influence. These are the thoughts harbored by those privileged whites in the higher social status and circles of socio-economic wealth that understand the true nature of the black man and woman. Due to generations of mistreatment of the descendants of the black once physical slaves, the new crop of Euro-ethnic leadership could for a while enjoy a measure of comfort. Only up until the day that the black man and woman began to make contact and connection with a substantial & reasonably accurate historical foundation. Today this body of knowledge, is labeled by black people living in America, as resurrection material. Information of this nature, is essential to giving a people sight who were once blinded, by the deceit of their oppressors conditioning, school systems, and media.

Fear tactics of Willie Lynch and those who studied and implemented his methods of control. Were based on a deeply imbedded internal fear for their life. Their abuse of their human property, caused within their own psyche layers of unstable security, which in internal response created an even greater emotional need within themselves to put more fear on their already destroyed human property. It was during those moments in history that the African who was being made a slave suffered another level of psychic terror never suffered before or after on long term scale recorded in human existence. As a reminder of what has occurred to the black family in general, we must express the level of psychological murder in the most minute detail as possibly provided by the English language. Even though words don't always qualify to equate the terror, we can come close by teaching what we know of true history. These are a couple of excerpts from the historical slave making document.

For example, take the case of the wild stud horse, a female horse and and already infant horse and compare the breaking process with two captured nigger males in their natural state, a pregnant nigger woman with her infant offspring. take the stud horse, break him for limited containment. Completely break the female horse until she becomes very gentle whereas you have the desired offspring. Then you can turn the stud to freedom until you need him again. Train the female horse whereby she will eat out of your hand, and she will in turn train the infant horse to eat out of your hand also.

When it comes to breaking the uncivilized nigger, use the same process, but vary the degree and step up the pressure so as to sow a complete reversal of the mind. Take the meanest and most restless nigger, strip him of his clothes in front of the remaining male niggers, the female, and the nigger infant, tar and feather him, tie each leg to a different horse in opposite directions, set him a-fire and beat both horses to pull him apart in front of the remaining niggers. The next step is to take a bullwhip and beat the remaining nigger male to the point of death in front of the female and the infant. Don't kill him, but put the fear of God in him, for he can be useful for future breeding.

Authors comment: The second and most popular Euro-ethnic expression of their fears was to castrate the penis and neuter the testicles of the black male in the very eyes of his offspring and the black woman. After he had been used as a breeding stud. Earlier we discussed the historical pattern of the reversal of the roles of gender in the chapter called Fixing Marriages & Breaking Old Social Cycles. In breaking any cycle one must locate the center point in which a cycle revolves. In the case of the black family it has been around one; the conditional mental loyalty to sacrifice black life in the form of spirit, labor, love, and self rejection for the sole benefit of pleasing the man who made us call him master. Only through a refreshing review of our mental history can this aspect of our database be re-built to the level that it can serve the black mind in rehabilitating its own faculties to the point where the individual unites with their higher self. The higher self represents the God element in the human being often times classified as the subconscious or the super ego. A plane where supreme guidance replaces general reasoning, will allow the black man and woman to break free from 446 years of hell and rise to the top over night.

Chapter Eight
Black Family Success During The Segregation Era

Let us review the history of early post slavery and the surrounding conditions, in comparison with the segregation era leading up to the time of de-segregation. In between then and now, something more unusual occurred within the framework of the black family structure and community as a whole. In this section our aim is to pinpoint legislation tied to Euro-centered social policies that have been used to support methods like Willie Lynch's mind controlling doctrine aiding in the process of making slaves.

In my studies I ran across a very interesting writing about a unique town entirely populated and governed by black people. For this aspect of the subject matter you will be asked to locate a book called "KINLOCH, Missouri's First Black City," written & documented by John A. Wright Sr., which is part of the Black America Series. This book was not picked as a reference point because it was my place of birth, but because of the unique social attitude of the state of Missouri, which happened to be the last state to set free their slaves.

I have found Mr. John A. Wright's book to be one of profound proof through example captured on pages as the perfect point of reference for this section in breaking the curse of Willie Lynch. In review we will discover the different shifts in the attitude of Black America over the many different shifts in the social climate of this country. Since black unity is a social matter, and the events produced by racism are social, we want to carefully observe the economic repercussions brought about by the era of integration & post segregation. Notice how the multi-faceted progressions and regressions of black people in North America.

For the sole purpose of provoking thought, I will ask you the reader a couple of questions in order to allow you to construct your own personal foundation, as a basis for breaking the curse of Lynch and company. During the time in which we presently exist in America, did black people gain more power and control over their destiny during the era of integration, than during the segregation era? Yes or No? What are the moral and economic down falls in the black communities in this country as a result of so called De segregation based on the theoretical promise of social equality with white society? How does the moral and economic condition of black men and women today, compare to the community actions and black moral social climate during the era of segregation?

From the time when the abolition of physical slavery took place up to the time of the civil rights movement, there seems to have been a backward shift in community consciousness in the mind state of Black America. Before the social de-segregation of Black and White America, black people had taken up the responsibility of developing our own educational systems. Even though blacks were segregated, we did not put social equality in front of black life quality. Quality education meant that blacks in their own school systems would demand proper curriculum materials even though they were under the influence of white scholarship. The three R's: Reading, Riting, and Rithimatic were supplied to inquiring young minds in our community.

Due to hundreds of years of anti-self, social conditioning combined with modern Euro-centric influence, education reform among black youth requires a much deeper penetration of the psychological realm in order to pierce the veil of falsified social barriers forged by policy and education under the mask of social integration. What we need, as a people, is inner black social integration, which is the infusion of all of the different divisions, organizations, political and religious persuasions into one clear constructive conglomerate.

This concept of organizing seemed to be very effective during the segregation era when black people had been totally shut out from white racist America. The leadership in the black community possessed some measure of personal power simply due to the harsh nature of the social circumstances; that time period provided no alternative to self-reliance. In contrast to the social incorporating of blacks into America's mainstream, the segregation era provided a certain amount of force, necessary to stimulate and up-root much of the superficial divisions listed in the documented letter of Lynch; because the level of pain produced by the high level oppression during that era in history. The circumstances of those time's forcing black people to work in a constructive manner in order to meet the basic requirements of every day survival. Overriding the implanted psychological divisions based on the training implemented by slave masters that used Willie Lynch's slave making sociology.

By being freed physically and allowed to think and function away from the plantation, black men and women discovered several key loop holes in past slave social conditioning. One was that the divisions were not as important as survival of the collective; In early post slavery we were recognized even according to Euro-gentile standards as being a separate independent people. Secondly blacks were in between a rock and a hard place because we were forced to choose to wrangle over old white imposed social standards of value such as size, age, shade, education, and wealth; contrary to the post slavery era when the choice was life or death. Presently, we live in an era of social de-segregation, were the implementation of an alternative social and economic view was provided through legislation. These Laws are now used   to maintain white dominated society by maintaining control over the modern slaves who had now become more mobile.

Control in relation to black liberation refers to the ability to influence, guide, or persuade aside from the input of another people's view. The author John A. Wright Sr. in his documentary "KINLOCH: Missouri's First Black City," captured a time in America's history that showed insurmountable economic growth and black inner racial integration with black progress before we became addicted to the falsely fabricated alternative, which today is called Civil Rights. This is a social code word that has historically proven to undermine any type of real substantial black self-empowerment. True self-empowerment has always blossomed from a people's ability to come together first with their own race and family, producing a culture and exemplary way of civilization, and then share those ideals with the rest of humanity.

During the segregation era, when black churches were collectively organized for the purpose of developing a school system using the Bible as a liberating tool and as a device of creating our own moral educational standard. This was a very effective method because by using what we were given from the slave master for our own purpose black people at that time were able to create an alternative that was very constructive in the arena of developing a system of education that catered specifically to our needs. Since the school system and the black churches at that time were connected, we were automatically in ownership of entire school districts. If you notice dwindling black owned schools immediately after the implementation of government de-segregation polices. As a collective, blacks were subtly lured away from personal community development for the sake of some mere so-called social advancement's that were supposed to come along with the package of integration. But only decades later did many black people come to realize that dropping the idea of black unity to become absorbed by the white unified and organized majority was a painful lesson.

Thanks to the era of segregation black people immediately began to make true human progress in the areas of business development, farming, product development, manufacturing, and most importantly, a solid family structure. A type of value system, which is the basis of society; family, which is an institution that has been destroyed from the kidnapping of the first African. Even then the African retained an understanding of the importance of family values, and a will to attempt to re-organize during the plantation era. But something changed dramatically for that first generation of Africans after breeding millions of new fresh fertile minds for the master. The entire generation of adults were murdered, leaving behind a race of orphans, that were now subject to the teaching, norms, and values of their captures. And for over three complete centuries under the tutelage of illegitimate foster parents. Only after the emancipation of physical bondage did black men and women have the opportunity to develop families outside of the influence of their former masters.

To expound on the pressure of segregation as a device of stimulus for black people after slavery in the area of self-help action aside from government programs, is the damage done by influential legislation that made it unlawful to incorporate prayer in the schoolroom. These policies uniquely were implemented during a time where black communities and their churches were gaining massive ground in school ownership. Then came a governmental assisted politically undermining curriculum. This is the input that played an important role in putting a stop to that part of black progress. Soon after, came the integration of schools, which divided the black community into separate districts. These are the events that finally led to the thinning out and watering down of black communities all over the United States.

Before the era of integration, black people in America had an overall better spiritual foundation than we did after de-segregation policies had been approved. What happened? We did not give up God, Church or Faith, so how all of a sudden did the reoccurrence of the Willie Lynch mentality emerge up out of the minds of black people causing us to sabotage our own families, and communities? Only when we reconnected in the relationship with the people who had, kidnapped, mistreated, murdered, divorced and psychologically raped you, did the principles in the Willie Lynch letter become effective in the life of black men and women.

Well black people, today we are not only in their house, but we realize that it is their house. Even though the Euro-gentile obtained his house through unfair schemes of actions, and falsification of deeds. It's impossible to rule your own life completely in what is defined as another man's house. Time to get into developing, real estate, agribusiness, chemistry, and engineering. But make sure that you are taking action after re-defining the value of which nation you are building for. Again, who's world are you building?

Chapter Nine
Re-Defining The New Black Reality

We have all heard the phrase "the power of the spoken word," but to what degree do we understand the impact of this concept? One culture may view such wording one way, and another culture may perceive the same phrase in an entirely different light. These perceptions are predominately determined based on that cultures ability, motive, and method used to define meanings relative to their reality. The scope of that vision determines the range of that specific people's level of freedom. As noticed by now, Willie Lynch and those who used similar methodologies to control the mind's of enslaved Africans were clear in defining the new reality of their African slave. Comprehension of the power to define, then re-define a new black reality by not only breaking old cycles, but to bring accurate insight to all intrigued by the magnetism of definitions, and their subtle powers.

Slavery as an institution made familiar to the African during that period of time, gave an obvious physical or carnal understanding of control, due to earthly barbaric treatment of the human anatomy of the captured African. The only difference between historical slavery in America is not necessarily the time, or treatment of black people, but our degree of tolerance based on the acceptance of custom designed

Euro-gentile definitions. Crafted to psychologically intoxicate the black mind to accept un-natural circumstances, and living conditions masked by passive aggressive Euro-gentile definitions.

The last 446 years of the Black reality has been masked and defined by laymen, religious circles, and social scientist, who were all well aware, that ultimate deception could be masked through shaping the slave minds perception of reality, while at the same time distorting the true meaning of key words necessary for the children of the once bound slave to ever liberate their own minds.

True power, is based on a people's ability to initiate a plan of constructive action based on their own definitions. It does not matter what the predominately larger social norms are, due to the fact that we are another people already defined by our own reality. This reality is based upon a completely different standard defined by those who determined that black people were different from those of European descent. Today more than ever before black men & women in America must re-define the one word that has been given to us by those who not only defined, but took it away from us. That word is freedom; and freedom to some does not mean freedom to all. Freedom of mobility, choice of employment, choice of relationships, and choice of residence all sound wonderful, but what constructive use are they if at the core of our understanding of freedom is one that only reflects or mimics another culture's definition?

Never before on the pages of history has another nationality, been so completely consumed by another culture's ways. My question to you is that even after being 140 years free from chains, why are we as a collective, so fragmented? The answer is simple! One nation has defined for another nation, it's position; and that one nation being black people who have accepted their assigned position based on what was defined for them.

Further detail of the definition of freedom can best be expressed by simply comparing Willie Lynch's people, and the offspring of those captured Africans that move about somewhat freely throughout this country. Freedom to the Euro-gentile is to roam the earth, build giant companies, set up governments & military bases in other countries, destroy any one who dares not to comply, and forcibly draft any one at any given time to do their bidding. On the other hand freedom as perceived and defined for blacks in this country is to reap the material scraps from the rewards of the Euro-gentiles freedom, and at the same time believe that they are reaping the benefits of true freedom. Simply because under the system of North American styled slavery we have been made to view another man's definition of freedom as if it completely applies to our particular set of circumstances. Here are documents on controlling the definitions of language, and are stated by slave makers as follows:

Cross breeding completed, for further severance from their original beginning, we must completely annihilate the mother tongue to both the new nigger and the new mule and institute a new language that involves the new life's work of both. You know that language is a peculiar institution. It leads to the heart of a people. The more a foreigner knows about the lan-

guage of another country the more he's is able to move through all levels of that society. Therefore, if the foreigner is an enemy of another country, to the extent that he knows the body of language, to that extent is the country vulnerable to attack or invasion of a foreign culture. For example, you take a slave, if you teach him all about your language, he will know all your secrets, and he is then no slave, for you can't fool him any longer, and being a fool is one of the basic ingredients to the slavery system.

For example if you told a slave that he must perform in getting out "our crops" and he knows the language well, he would know that "our crops" didn't mean "our crops", and the slavery system would break down, for he would relate on the basis of what "our crops" really meant. So you have to be careful in setting up the new language for the slave would soon be in your house, talking to you as "man to man", and that is death to our economic system. In addition, the definition of words or terms is only a minute part of the process. Values are created and transported by communication through the body of the language. A total society has many interconnected value systems. All these values in the society have bridges of language to connect them for orderly working in the society. But for these language bridges, these many values systems would shapely clash, and cause internal strife or civil war, the degree of the conflict being determined by the magnitude of issues of relative opposing strength in whatever form. For example, if you put a slave in a hog pen and train to life there and incorporate in him to value it as a way of life completely, the biggest problem you would have out of *him is that he would worry you about provisions to keep the hog pen clean, or partially clean, or he might not worry you at all. On the other hand, if you put this same slave in the same hog pen and make him slip and incorporate something in his language where by he comes to value a house more than he does his hog pen, you got a problem. He will soon be in your house.*

Chapter Ten
The Origin & Ending
Of
Self Hate

In order to successfully ensure an end to the self hate which is the foundation of dis-unity, the old plantation education received, by black men and women during our early enslavement as a collective must be defined as racially counter-productive. Comparing the black man and woman of America to other organized nations around the globe, we find no other people with such a peculiar type of psychological basis for socializing with one another. Within the mental perimeters of the so-called freed slave lies the oppressor's idea of a crippling self sabotage behavior.

These actions can be traced back to what is known as the crabs in the barrel mentality. When one black person strives to serve a cause higher than the typical norm set for the betterment of the whole, the rest of the crabs in the barrel instinctively disapprove. Strive to be something other than a servant of the opponent's system, and you'll find yourself being hated by your own kind on the same level as expressed through the man who by nature showed the African no love. So where did this type of thinking stem from? Is self hatred now a chemically fixated part of black men and women in America? If so, what has happened as a result of past social training that we as a people have not noticed in our investigation through psychology, genetics and Afro-centered social sciences?

First and foremost we will have to understand the detrimental genetic effects of the chemistry that the African in America has encountered through involuntary, and voluntary race mixing. This is one of the missing factors in terms of understanding why it is so difficult for black people to trust, unite, love one another, and productively organize to build any thing of surmountable value outside of service to the children of the former slave masters. Before expounding on this aspect of our subject any further, ask yourself do you understand why the slave master raped and used cross breeding on the pure blooded African? First of all what is the true definition of crossbreeding? According to Webster's Dictionary, **crossbreed:** an individual or breed produced by the crossing of different varieties or, more rarely species. **Cross:** means to pervert, thwart; oppose; go counter to: 4:to pass over from one chromosome to another that is homologous: said of chromatin material in a gene of factor. In order for us to go any further we must clearly define the word **chromosome:** the microscopic rod-shaped bodies into which the chromatin <u>separates</u> during mitosis: they carry the genes that convey hereditary characteristics. Review the following information recorded on slave making that documents the motive of slave making through the creation of black-on-black self hate.

Cross-breeding niggers means taking as many drops of good white blood and putting them into as many nigger women a possible, varying the drops by various tones that you want, and then letting them breed with each other until the circle of colors appear as you desire. What this means is this: Put the niggers and the horse in the breeding pot, mix some asses and some good white blood and what do you get? You got a multiplicity of colors of ass backward, unusual niggers, running, tied to backward ass long-headed mules, the productive of itself, the other sterile (the one constant, the other dying --we keep the nigger constant for we may replace the mule for another tool) both mule and nigger tied to each other, neither knowing where the other came from and neither productive for itself, nor without each other.

When observed the above is just as physically noticeable in the United States of America as it is in South Africa where you have an entire segment of the population called colored. The meaning of the word colored means something totally opposite to what black people have traditionally been made to think. When the suffix "ed" is placed on the end of color, which signifies the past state of a noun or verb after the occurrence of certain action. In reference to crossbreeding the word "colored" has a *hormonal* effect, which means having the nature of, and is derived from the greek word horme, impulse. The significance beneath the surface of these definitions as they relate to the intention of the slave master is to produce internal conflict within the black psyche through contaminating the black slave genetically with the inception of Euro-gentiles DNA on a bio-chemical level.

Not only is the bio-engineering of different shades necessary to create a psychotic self-hate race war among the black slave population necessary during the days of physical bondage; but today is reinforced socially through de-segregation formally known as racial integration. This illusion is another aspect of century old control methods used by every Pharaoh throughout history, which is the intermingling of the emotions through alleged social gains from wanting the material benefits that come along with uniting and defending the economic kingdom of the oppressor.

Chapter Eleven
The Black Widow: Healing The Wounds Of The Black Woman

The Red Back spider, which is one of the early names affiliated with this peculiar creature now called the Black Widow, will be used in metaphorical fashion, because its relationship among its own species best describes the nature of black male/female relationships as a result of North American slave making techniques. When the list of differences mentioned in the Willie Lynch letter were used to create division among the black slave, the most practiced and effective difference was the different nature of the male and female. In essence these are two natures that under normal circumstances without interruption would complement one another harmoniously.

As a basis for properly concluding this writing let us ask ourselves, what is the significance of the spider on the front cover of this book? In the process we will define in detail the curse of Willie Lynch in a manner that will allow us to clearly see through the web of social chaos which serves as a trap for black people in North America. We have already discussed earlier the slave making system of Willie Lynch and others of his like mind, that perfectly understood the natural structure of the roles of leadership and responsibility communicated between male and female within the framework called a family unit.

In studying the nature of the Black Widow spider I made an interesting comparison to the end results -stemming from the Willie Lynch method. Firstly let us define the word "Widow" outside of typical belief of what the word describes on the surface. Widow 1. is of course a woman who has outlived the man to whom she was married at the time of his death: especially, such a woman who has not remarried. 2. In certain card games, and extra hand dealt to the table, such as the trump card. 3. and most importantly to deprive or bereave of something valued is to widow. *Bereave:* which means to deprive; to strip; to leave destitute; to deprive, as by death: with of before the person or thing taken away: as bereaved of a father, mother, or child; 2 to take away from, to strip.

During slavery the Euro-gentile slave maker trained the black female to be dominant and to turn over possession of the black infant child especially the more passively trained black male slave to the white authority. This old archaic occurrence is presently flourishing in the minds and actions of black men and women in North America. This aspect of black male/female behavior acts as a poison to the whole unit, due to being fed through the slavery process in small quantities in the form of harmful emotions of tyranny and competition trough jealously, which is destructive to happiness and the general welfare of a race. This poison can also be defined as the wrongful influence exhibited by the corrupting of the black mind brought about by centuries of deceitful leadership.

The title "Breaking The Curse Of Willie Lynch" is given as a curse due to the old archaic karma that has followed over from generation to generation in a cycle that needs to be broken. Therefore the circumstance surrounding the black man and woman could be classified not only as un-natural but a curse, which is defined as to subject to evil or inflict injury on a person. The entity of Lynch's curse exists in the sub-conscious mind and is carried out by and presently lives in the black material reality. This mind reproduces, and lives on stronger due to the nature of its design which survives based on the existence of the single black female, whether single or married, is still considered a widow, because her male counter-part of the species like the black widow male lacks potency or power. A woman without a man of power fits the classification of black widow because a man without adequate power is considered one of the living-dead.

Being alive yet in the dark, or not illuminated by the light of understanding puts the black man and woman in a similar condition to the time period called the Dark Ages where lack of true progress and ignorance prevailed. The ignorance that is carried on among millions of black men and women is exactly as planned by Willie Lynch in the year of 1712. And finally this is why the Black Widow spider was used on the cover because historically they are synonymous with curses, mysticism and things of a like nature. But mostly because the nature of the male, and female of this particular species perfectly describes and parallels with the un-natural aspect of the circumstances among black men and women in North America. The male is passive and the female of this species is extremely aggressive, and the male is primarily only used for mating. Just like the Black Widow female spider that is unquestionably the more dominant half of the species. She is also known to be aggressive after mating, and has a notorious propensity to turn on, devour, and eat the non venomous male after the mating.

The role reversal as implemented by Willie Lynch's is a technique as old as the one that Pharaoh used during the time of Moses in the Bible where the newborn males were to be killed (physically or mentally) and the economic sparing of the female in that society ironically parallels with the black male in this society today as reflected in the un-natural nature of the female reference to Black Widow Spiders.

There are several major obstacles that black people in America must overcome before rising to the next level of progress and cultural consciousness. The tackling of these psychological obstacles are of profound importance to the black race overall, but especially for the black woman. The overall success of our present condition and discussion involves her investment on a very deep spiritual level. If we as men and women are the product of a culture giving birth to a set of odd shaped circumstances, due to the nature of our arrival to this point in time. We must ask our selves several questions about Willie Lynch including those who were possessed by his state of mind.

What did Mr. Lynch and other slave masters understand about the nature of women in their relationship to power? Secondly, how do modern black women who aren't aware of these old control methods executed on the black slaves on the plantation, presently reflect and manifest the masters intended reactions in modern day relationships? Third, how can an entire nation of people be helped by legislation when the female is being used as a political pawn to aid in the demise of family in the name of government assistance? Finally how would black men and women benefit as a collective from a more black-survival approach to the institution of marriage? And one of the other issues on the board relative to breaking the old habits of mimicking another people's culture and way of organizing family structures, mostly centered around vain egotistical motives, superficially created values and Euro-centric self centered motives when dealing with one another as black men and women. As an author, it is my responsibility to seek and discover truth while reflecting on the hand that history has dealt our people.

Theologically speaking white males have always understood from a biblical standpoint that the woman was and is the help meet to her husband.. In other words the caucasian knows that the nature of women under healthy circumstances is to support their men and help his guidance manifest divinity. So to rule a nation securely without the major loss of physical life, the Euro-gentile set forth a plan of mastery of the black woman. Control of the black female slave was implemented first and foremost to effect total control of the black male slave, because the only way to rule a man mentally without open conflict is through the one thing by nature he was designed to love unconditionally; his African Woman! Otherwise the only way to non-violently rule a man is to do so through wielding influence over the mind of his woman combined with training the black male mind to function in a subjectively passive manner. Using the Willie Lynch document and others like it as point of reference, we as black men and woman will both be able to break the curse of Willie Lynch. Read the slave masters comments about, this aspect of our subject matter is as follows.

Then take the female run a series of tests on her to see if she will submit to your desires willingly. Test her in every way because she is the most important factor for good economics. If she shows any sign of resistance in submitting completely to your will, do not hesitate to use the bullwhip on her to extract the last bit of bitch out of her. Take care not to kill her; for in doing so, you spoil good economics. When in complete submission, she will train her offspring in the early years to submit to labor when they become of age.

The above statements are true by action based on the supporting social circumstances and the loyalty of the female to government handouts. Putting money in her pocket book creates a subconscious alliance between the black female indirectly with the white male, which serves as a guise of white power in the name of black female security. In turn the power of the will of young males raised by females have in turn no legitimate legal choice but to be turned over to the system. From a historical view, this is the standard pattern of action created on the plantation that is still expressed through the black female today, especially through overprotection of the black male child. For example read what the Willie Lynch letter & The making of a slave documented as follows, and ask yourself: are there any noticeable patterns consistent with the economic labor established during the days of forced physical slavery?

Before the breaking process, we had to be alertly on guard at all times. Now we can sleep because his woman stands guard for us. He cannot get past her infant slave training process. He is a good tool; now ready to be tied to the horse at a tender age.

By the time a Nigger reaches the age of sixteen, he is soundly broken in and ready for life's sound and efficient work and the reproduction of a unit of good labor force. Continually, though the breaking of uncivilized savage niggers, by throwing the nigger female savage into a frozen psychological state of independencies, by killing off the protective male by creating a submissive dependent mind of the nigger male savage, we have created an orbit that turns in its own axis forever, unless a phenomenon occurs and reshifts the positions of the female savages.

*Will You Help
Continue The Cycle Of Willie Lynch's Curse On Your Kind*

Chapter Twelve
The De-Magnification Of Ego

Throughout the process of the un-doing of a slave mentality, the once physical slave must come to realize the importance of harmony in relationships. A harmony, that can only be brought about through the balancing of ego. When we speak of balanced ego, we are including the individual's natural tendency to represent it self, which in psychoanalysis is the part of the psyche that distinguishes the developed identity, experiences the external through the senses, and subconsciously controls the impulses of the individual. Based on the conditioning of the black ego during the slave making process, the natures of the black man & woman were perverted from their proper use, and natural expression. So much to the degree that the feminine, and masculine energies of the black conscious ego today seeks expression from competition, by feeding on sources outside of it's original internal self. This is the problem in many of today's black male/female relationships that have overlapped from the age-old "divide and manipulate" method, mentioned in the Willie Lynch Letter.

In order to gain a proper perspective on this subject matter, let us reflect that during the slave making process, every intention was to weaken, distort, and destroy the Ego, self- estimation, and natural expectations of the black slaves inherent ability to create and shape reality for itself. While the Euro-slave-makers were breaking the black ego, they were creating false illusions of self importance within certain individual slaves based on the black slaves duties. For example, even Two Hundred and Ninety-two years from the indoctrination of the principles documented in the Willie Lynch letter, many of our people still base their self importance, and success on their close affiliation with their service to their corporate masters. From this position the weakened ego begins to connect to itself importance based on status, competition, and the devaluation of those who don't have, versus those that do. As mentioned in the making of a slave document, once the slave's mind can contact a substantial historical base, the mind will and has the tendency to correct and re-correct itself. This law works equally with the damaged ego, in that under attack or underdeveloped, it automatically asserts itself in order to compensate for any of its own shortcomings.

In the case of the African brought to the Americas during the physical bondage process, families were fragmented, and torn apart. The destruction of African historical evidence only compounded the problem of the dis-empowered black male, and the symbolically assisted black female during the era of affirmative action through the civil rights movement. Therefore in balancing the magnified ego that now aids in the break down of black families, we must also realize that the Ego in black men and women must not only have connections with spirituality but is also synonymous with history. In other words, this is where the connection of a people's physical history, their biological accomplishments, and visual cultural customs are brought into the picture connecting them with their mental history. Only then can the self be repaired, expressed and communicated to the outside world in a harmonious manner.

Another important element that the skilled makers of slaves realized is the difference between mental history, which are the human developmental arts, and sciences, such as meditation, yoga's, prayer technique, spirituality and clean dieting. These sciences contain the mathematical basis for the manifestation of our ancient historical accomplishment, that physically records it self on the pages of history. Once black men and women can be educated in the mathematical mental sciences practiced to develop the inner-man, along with clearing the amnesia of our recorded physical past, and then connecting these two aspects of our existence can we properly channel the natural energies of the mis-directed slave ego.

Let us modernize this concept of demagnetizing the damaged ego, and bring it directly up to the present moment and see how the music industry and it's artist are unconsciously feeding the ego of the black masses in a manner that creates a falsified form of self esteem for the privileged boastful few; to those they view as subject. While at the same time these artist brag about material gain, and are still subject and powerless to the companies owned by the same people who owned and conditioned their fore-parents generations before. These artist have more than enough money to acquire legitimate power, control, and distribution, of radio airwaves in the most influential area of the public: the media. This powerlessness is largely due to the misdirecting of their egos, mistaking luxury and fame, which are the illusive symbols of power. Contradicting the reality currently existing defined as the damaged slave ego, which in most cases has not been properly developed in themselves.

Today the ego of the once physical slave is fed constantly through the media's entertainment, and advertisement giants trough the over stimulation and focus on sex. Not much different from controlled breeding methods of the black man and woman during the days of plantation life. Black men were considered valuable to the ruling class based on his production of numerous litters of black babies for the purpose of slave economics. Not being required or even allowed to partake in the slightest bit of responsibility, he was rewarded by the slave maker with the classification title "Stud". Today these type of money making black males still carry the physical load are symbolically privileged, and called "Professional Athletes". Two hundred and ninety-one years from the date on the Willie Lynch document, black men are still drafted and traded from institution to institution, and from team (plantation) to team (plantation) whether they choose to or not.

The egotistical activity of black celebrities, are mimicked, by those being entertained on the other side of the big screen. Differing only from the influential people in the spotlight in that they really don't have the financial means to support the weight of the over-magnified-ego like the celebrities. Black men and women are unconsciously participating in the Eurocorporate media's economic strategy to create the insecurity of "not having", as psychologically not being established in the world as one of those possessing less value. If we look back into the words of the making of a slave document, and the earlier chapters in this book, we would come to the conclusion that the manipulation of a destroyed black ego for at least three centuries was only the preliminary ground work for today's modern economy. For this economy has only survived based upon the foundation of black labor, energy, and fear. These three essentials combined with the manipulation of a low-esteemed ego only further's the division between black men and women. The potency of Willie Lynch's age old method further intensifies black disunity, when fed and magnified based on the concept and action of continued material consumption.

Chapter Thirteen
The End Of Envy
&
Black Slave Classism

From the realm of the magnified ego comes the bi-product of envy and classism. This happens when our egos begin to attribute to themselves value based on material visibles, while at the same time comparing themselves in the spirit of conceit to those whose egos have not been established before the view of the physical eye. When the ego of those whose material accomplishments, or personal level of public appeal does not compete with the next persons material success, then that culture becomes contaminated with the dis-ease of envy and classism. From a position of government and authority these human shortcomings can be created, and stimulated for the purpose of control. Especially when the creation of falsified differences are given value, and made noticeable to the outward seeing eye!

After nearly 300 years of Euro-conditioning, and anti-self socializing combined with black peoples over indulgence in materialism, two elements surface and prevail. One being distinguished as a paid labor pool of people who are addicted to consumption based on a fear frozen ego, and the other being an apparently secure ethnic class of people who are the beneficiaries of cycled out dollars based on black consumer addiction to "recreational goods" more so than progressive needs. On the surface mass consumption of material products just sounds like day today business, simply because that's what the physical eye sees. Lying beneath the surface are the elements of surprise resulting in two separate economic classes; one class obtains the symbols of wealth, power, and influence. The other economic class is properly educated, functional, and engrossed in the reality of true power. The "haves" and those who appear to have, is a result of the illusions mentioned in the excerpts from other parts of the slave document.

Akin to the insecure ego's on both sides of the class equation is "Envy" a spiritual dis-ease that sublimely manifests outwardly through human form in an antagonistic function working against the grain of the next person's accomplishments. In reference to relationships, it is the ego's left sided expression to equalize or compensate for class differences whether the differences are imposed from an outside source, physically visible, or imagined. As black men and women we must scientifically understand the duality of classism and envy from within the framework of our own homes. The offspring produced from the seeds of division is a subtle, yet an unconscious power struggle that often takes place between male & female. Struggles for the next persons energy are common in relationships, but due to slave conditioning applied on the African brought to the western world severely complicates the situation. Competition for energy through the manipulation of emotions for acquiring attention, is common in human relationships in general, but produces division in the end. Silent, passive aggressive attempts for influence slowly begin to boil over into the emotionally quarrelsome communications between the ego starved individuals. This dilemma is sublimely present within each person. Now you have a fight on your hands, because all along the emotional waters were being boiled by the ego to see which locomotive was going to lead by proving that it can blow off the most steam.

Without the influence of deliberate outside forces, these normal circumstances can be changed for the better through normal counseling. The creative purpose of the planetary astrological influences, that shapes the individuals characteristics while they are being fashioned in the womb. Astro-science should be used as a tool for self-diagnosis, and not to permanently fix or attribute to ones character a negative trait that needs to be adjusted. To do so would be to paralyze the developmental process in the individual. In breaking the curse of Willie Lynch, the planetary Astro-sciences should never be ignored when in the process of healing, building a relationship, or when analyzing the spiritual make up of ones self. For it is true that every individual will, and has the inherent ability to excel further than every other human being in some field of human endeavor based on their special God given talent. The mathematical and Astro-sciences can, if used properly will aide each person who uses them to discover their talents, life path and personal lessons.

When individuals have a complete knowledge of self, the ego's energies are constructively directed, in a proper manner. Then that individual's talents, and characteristics blossom manifesting their, naturally distinguished state of growth belonging only to themselves. In this state black men and women can begin to express the love developed in ourselves: for our community abroad. Only after every individual in the black community does the self analysis systems check & treats their self of the conditions produced by the Willie Lynch epidemic, can we achieve the fruits of true freedom.

Chapter Fourteen
Empowering Black Relationships

By knowing the nature, circumstances, and slave making methods that laid the basis for black male/female relationships during the North American slavery experience, can Black America as a collective begin to up-root the foundation of our division. Such a process would fall under the self-developmental arts. These arts would clear our minds of Euro-centric influences, and at the same time would re-cultivate the damaged essence of each individual's very being. To magnify the perception of this idea by exemplifying the process of meditation on a nation wide level, where black people would psychologically, educationally, and culturally detach from feeding off of the product of our division for at least one week. No television, radio, entertainment, or sport & play for that one week. This week of nation wide meditation, and dialogue would include the black family only. Why the isolation? Because during the practice of silent stillness comes the correct answers, and universal guidance. In contrast how can you communicate in a room cluttered with noise equal to a thousand people talking at one time? It's almost impossible to relate clearly under such circumstances: while at the same time black people are using the antagonistic dogma of our former slave masters as the foundation for our relationships with one another.

This meditative method is also inclusive of the deliberate separation of western ideology as opposed to the acceptance of an eastern Afro-centric value system. A criterion inclusive of the very people for whom by nature these practices were designed to sustain, and advance. In other words black men and women who have undergone 400 years of foreign forced indoctrination must discontinue going to the same source that made us sick, as if that source would yield the proper medicine for our illness. Poison on top of poison equals more poison, which is exactly what the Willie Lynch letter taught when it said that after one year would become self-refueling among the indoctrinated Negro slaves. Some black men and women in attendance have stood the test of time in their relationships, and therefore may not see the relevance of the idea of a black nation in meditation. One might think that their family is successful in that there is a mutual harmony among its functioning members, but family at this point takes on another turn and responsibility extending to the larger community. Almost a duplicate of a business franchise system, or a multi-level marketing network, where other successfully functioning components organize and begin to empower through numbers, expansive action, and building momentum collectively in their desired direction.

Before such an empowering idea can be manifested, the total reassessment of the black approach to validating legitimate relationships, that recognize, the security and control of the balance of power concerning the individuals involved. Power is an issue of security in every type of relationship, and is of a more serious concern when the subject of marriage is being considered. Today, many marriages have become reduced to the sole idea of economic security, when nearly 40 years ago the union was justified as a moral issue. A time now exists where black men who would commit to marriage, are afraid because of a state of economic castration, where it becomes unbearably painful to go through the drama of divorce court especially when children are conceived. And on the other end the black female in over 70 percent of the cases, are forced to become a single parent relying on whatever assistance can be gained form laws designed to protect and secure her. Black men and women must both reflect that law in nature is designed to regulate the lower characteristics in the human being. In brief, the children of chattel slaves must indeed master the laws of nature that will override laws of western man. For example if the African brought to North America has been and is still subject to a western moral standard, and has lost control of the available faculties to govern him self morally. What has to be understood? First, is that the law of nature is designed to empower, based on applying the principles and disciplines within the framework of a more higher universal power.

Man made laws, are derived from his chosen belief system. What is the present thought process supporting the laws that we as black men and women use to guide, and govern our attitudes about the institution of marriage? Furthermore are these original beliefs producing laws that work for the betterment or detriment of black unification? If not, we must be moral enough to develop a healthy trust between men and women in the black community. A moral code that is strong enough to break the influence of the civic laws surrounding marriage and control of black people today. Remember how we were trained to relate to one another through a breeding process in the fields of the plantation! First of all, why should marriage between two people ever become a three-way contract?

What we are witnessing is a state organization, controlled, & operated family management system, which stems from early North American Slave Economics. Today the average American citizen is affected by state controlled marriage contracts designed to capitalize on, and foster broken families creating a multi-billion dollar divorce industry. A government monopolized family law industry cannot function profitably without divorce mediation through legalized state authorization. This whole process is morally contradicting. Marriage is a sacred act through which people swear by God that they will remain in the relationship for better or for worse; but at the same time before a state appointed judge mediating the act. We live in an era where the church is supposed to be legally separate from the state. Based on the methodology of Willie Lynch these laws do not empower the men in the economic outcome in divorce, which means that they are crafted to indirectly dis-empower the black woman.

Based on statistics, the average male deciding to marry faces a 50% chance of divorcing within eight years. Chances are that most of his assets will be lost, and will be forced compulsively by the state in a non-negotiable manner to pay at least one third of his take home salary if there are children to support. For the average black male, this is merely a modern re-introduction into physical slavery. Through the government extracting his income or working for next to nothing in jail due to insufficient payments of child support in order to survive day to day. These laws are enforced as a one size fits all, which only creates major money problems simply due to the reality that individual income and living expenses vary in strength in comparison of one person to another. To empower the black family strength should not be dis-proportioned favoring one side over the other, because if so there is no real strength and solidarity with the family members when there is no balance in the equation. Marriage contracts should, and can be designed privately by the two individuals involved. Private marriage contracts can be drawn up between each party's consenting to all terms and clearly providing a complete disclosure of assets sealed and approved by a Notary Public. If not the contract is possibly subject to be overturned later. Marriage contracts must be honored in the courts even if the standard marriage license method is replaced by an alternative method. Contracts of this nature have not only empowered both parties during a possible dissolution of marriage, but have brought a better understanding of the terms of their expectations of one another. A process that teaches the practice of compromise, and negotiation before entering into a long term commitment. These types of marriage contracts are essential if black men and women are to acquire, enough power to gravitate toward the influence of our own system of relating to each other without the influence of our oppressor's children.

Chapter Fifteen

Reversing
Spiritual Homosexuality
&
Black Male Economic
Impotence

Through out history, Empires like America, Ancient Rome, Greece, & Babylon have always used the same method of dictatorship. That common thread that they all share is that they were only successful to the extent of their ability to de-maculate the subjected male aspect of the conquered population. As students of history we must observe certain guidelines in order to be successful. The first rule of observation to be mindful of is, that history best qualifies and rewards its researcher. For example, bible history gives us the example in the parable of Moses & Pharaoh where the oppressive authorities sent out systematic orders instructing their military officials to kill all boy babies. The slaughter of the boy babies was then and is now a form of population control. The Pharaoh during the era of Moses said come, let us deal wisely with them least they multiply, join on to an enemy of ours and come against us.

How was, Willie Lynch and the North American method of mind control any different from her parent countries from which she and her people originated? The difference is that America is more technically advanced and possesses greater military manpower. Well then, how much more uniquely different must the men of this present day bi-product of modern day slave masters be if he is to break the curse of servitude? In earlier chapters we mentioned that the only difference between the Negro slave during pre-emancipation and post physical slavery was that today's modern Negro has fancy transportation, is allowed to be more mobile, and is free to choose their own plantation, and is comfortable existing as such in comparison to the Negro slave of yesterday. The answer to the second question is relatively the black mans advantage thanks to time, and the struggles of the many freedom fighters who have lead us up to this moment. The advantage is that there are no physical chains; the main restraints are ignorance & fear. Trauma imposed through centuries of unjust violence, that has scared the black man and woman, on a deep spiritual level.

Over time the children of slaves have evolved to progress in areas before not imagined, but definitely not unnoticed by the offspring of former holders of black slaves. Today many Black men & women in this country have failed in that we have forgotten two things. One that we are the product of a white investment, and that investments as large as the one that we were made a part of are generational, residual, or what is commonly classified as long term investments. The second factor of our error is not realizing that the Negro emancipated by the hands of his oppressor was in fact, not functioning in that present state as he would have, if left intact with his original nature. What comes to mind when defining man in his original state? Today as defined by the average man through his economics, but in nature it is his ability to be creative through, the usefulness of his will to be self-productive.

Spiritual homosexuality is applied in its relation to the de-maculated black male slave. Refers to his un-natural state of dependence, and lack of economic productivity. Not only on the systems, programs, and policies of his oppressors, but to the female component of his culture. If we are living in the so-called age of independent women, where does the concept of a dependent male come from? Who supports this concept, and why? What are the long-term internal consequences, and their effects on the black family? And what civilized society can maintain it self under such circumstances? The entire organized world can see that the natural order of male/female in 80% of Black families in North America, are as awkward as a breached birth! These circumstances occur only when people of African origin conform to the norms, and ideology of the western white world. An ideal system, that by nature sets the tone for the destabilizing, and down fall of black family.

There must be a specific type of influenced education that stimulates spirit in, black men causing them to control their own reality in the areas of civilized industries, such as manufacturing, product distribution marketing, engineering, agriculture, and total control of the political scene in the black community. In relationships black men must connect with the God within, and make sure not ignore their intuitive vision which is more broader than mere material achievement. Black males in their youth instinctively know that there is something backwards in the training methods that they have received in the educational system. The traditional training that the disempowered single parent female often puts her faith in, is the same system that she was molded by during physical slavery. Black females received certain rights over the black male slave under those set conditions, that has shaped her perceptions, attitudes, and a controlled mode of authority treatment toward the male counter part of her race.

In order for black men in relationships to reverse this process, and at the same time avoid any further internal male/female conflict requires very astute understanding of the Willie Lynch program, development of skill in handling the self sabotaging female mind that has been Euro-synthesized. The first aspect to a solution here involves, mastering the English language, understanding the folly in western psychology in its application to the spiritual nature of African thought. Second, which is equally important is communicating without argument, which is obviously a sign of a sublime power struggle. Remember that argument is a form of control loss, either from within the individual provoking confrontation, or their ability to direct the energy of their partner. As men, never engage in argument with your black female this lowers your magnetic fields frequency, which automatically dulls your ability to attract the female in a non-compulsive manner.

Don't be scared to loose what you think you have, you are the Sun, and she is the Moon. As you create space to avoid confrontation, the male vibration escalates like the Suns gravity, while the Moon (Females) emotional state softens to the warmth of your radial energies, knowledge and divine guidance. Remember that beyond the principles in the Willie Lynch indoctrination are eternal natural laws working to re-correct our natural tendencies. One such law is the law of like attracts like. Every person in your history of your personal relationships, are but a gauge of your personal growth. In other words you are what you attract, which means that neither black man or woman is at direct fault. But at the same time we must be responsible enough to admit that the person we are involved with is only a reflection of our present state of development.

As black men you must see your reality clearly and understand that that by nature, even though the average black female may never admit, that they are subject to whoever is in power. She in her state of unconscious sleep, not knowing why she thinks the way that she thinks today submits to the structure of the white male. For example her Euro-synthetic independent posture produces men that are followers living in a dependent state of, in-activity. Black men must take an economic power move in all of the industries stated above. For example when looking at the Hip Hop Music Industry created and pioneered by Black men without judgment based on our personal opinion, look at their wealthy example. Even in a mass state of negativity, the hardcore street artist have attracted the attentive ear of the entire black generation, respect of female youth to the point where they are expressing themselves in a sexually un-dignifying manner, and created a multi-billion dollar clothing industry. These men negative or positive are on the right path with the right idea, and they have, the right intention. Freedom is the underlying principle! Lets work to evolve the moral of black media, because they are also in need of Breaking The Curse Of Willie Lynch

Chapter Sixteen
Recognizing Game

The final perquisite to bringing anything into the light is to be able to discover the true nature of that thing or person. This aspect of discovery is of great need in black relationships. Before going any further let's ask our selves what is the natural intent of game? And secondly who in the relationship is more than likely to gravitate toward initiating the game?

First of all to **Recognize** means to admit knowledge of the fact, being certain of the identification of a person as being known to one. In defining the word **game**; it is characterized as a scheme pursued in order to plot diversion, an act of un-willingness to take ones place in natural order, and to manipulate competitively. In the psychological realm to **game** means to go against or contest nature, to deceive ones very self with ones own intelligence, in street terms, to psych-your-self-out. Since we are dealing with the reality of Willie Lynches generational curse on black life in North America, we must admit openly and honestly to ourselves the truth of this matter at every turn. In doing so we will not unknowingly run a game on our self.

At this point a basic understanding of slave making methodology should be very clear. We can all agree that the reversal of roles in nature only warps orderly family structure. This truth also applies to the entire race, to the same extent as being a people who lack total self-reliance, which in its self is in contradiction by depending on another people to provide for us our employment, education, food, clothing and shelter. Not one black man or woman in America or the enslaved world over can escape the reality of this truth. Now how does the previous apply to recognizing game on a personal level? Getting us to admit the truth on a broader level, by not being so direct allows us to look at self with constructive criticism.

Male & Female relationships are governed by universal laws, that were set forth in divine creation to protect the entire human species. The woman is the second self of man, his feminine reflection, his subtle weaker, softer half, and in Biblical terms his helpmeet. Now every human being at some point in their lives has experienced the reality of being lied to by some one playing a game with some aspect of their life. Now lets bring this point to the forefront, because some men play games on women & some women play games on men. In the sports arena most times the object is to keep the ball in your possession or side of the court as much or many times as possible. And in most cases the ball is always moving or is the object subject to being controlled. In this example the term ball shall be replaced with, and symbolized with **energy**, which can be termed as **will**. It seems that the **ball** in any sport is the center focus of the rivaling competitors.

In many relationships today our conscious will and our energy are like the ball an object of focus and control. To reach an answer to the second question at the beginning of the chapter, who is more likely to initiate the game? It is the person in the relationship who carries more of the feminine qualities. Even though tradition would like us to always attribute this action to the woman, it is not always the case. The male half of the human species carries the (X & Y) Chromosome.

Based on the astrological sciences certain signs are defined as either feminine or masculine. Therefore it is not uncommon to for one to be observing of masculine traits in women. Notice that men or women are more feminine when possessing signs such as Taurus, Cancer, Virgo, Scorpio, Capricorn, Pisces, and are more masculine when possessing Aries, Gemini, Leo, Sagittarius and Aquarius. The Libra is both masculine & feminine. Another cosmic difference takes place involving the Pisces, because the male of this sign carries more feminine traits and the female carries more masculine traits. We brought this subject into discussion in order to gain clarity on unraveling the confusion propagated, by this slave making technique. Since our goal is to bring understanding, by showing the effect of these elements on human nature.

Observe that both Feminine & Masculine energies that subside as a duality in male nature can be easily dissected in their relativity to games. There are three things in life that every one desires. These three things being a part of the human psyche automatically spill over into our daily relationships. But due to Willie Lynches mind enslaving techniques, these three desires are magnified more largely in black male / female relationships. These three tendencies are, **Recognition, Control, & Security.**

With a little practice and simple observation you will notice, that one of the three common tendencies in human nature pre-dominate the personality of the people you come in contact with. You will be able to see their angle within the first Thirty seconds of conversation. The three are inter-woven meaning that a person seeking security will seek control to the extent of his or her insecurity. Secondly, a person who wants control will seek recognition to the extent that they emotionally feel they lack respect. Under normal observation this is phrased, as seeking attention or competing for attention. It is the feminine aspect of the ego that is more inclined to seek domination under oppressive or unjust circumstances. Since the feminine is representative of the emotional half of man (not necessarily male) it is the first to suffer being subject to domination, abuse, and subordination in any relationship. Under these circumstances female instinct normally seeks recognition or control to obtain security.

In black male/female relationships, the difficulty of a remedy involves complete acknowledgment of historical facts on Willie Lynches American partaking of Roman methods of controlling the African mind. The original African concept involves an honest admission of the role of man and woman in proper balance putting the man in the leading position in his home. **Black men need to take into strong consideration three questions when choosing a helpmeet. 1. Does she Love you for you? 2. Does she put her needs before yours? 3. Does she inspire you to seek your creator? The female must ask these same questions to her emotional feminine self as well as the**

masculine rational aspect of her psychological being. For women answering these questions to them selves, it serves as an exercise of mastering their feminine emotional element. If you have all three of these questions answered yes as a black male, you are more than likely in a harmonious relationship already, and have enough peace of mind to produce a prosperous family. Your woman has more than likely developed stronger faith, security, and pride in knowing that she is successful in being who she is and not necessarily what she can become.

CONCLUSION

As we mentioned in the beginning of this writing, this book dealt with the economic collapse of America. I made an attempt at an approach somewhat un-orthodox in that I focused on the historical mental conditioning of the black slave. The present American capitalist economy was successful, because of centuries of free black labor. Now, as a result of the training the vast majority of black men and women received on the plantation during American slavery. Black men & women after being physically freed still cooperate by converting 100% of our energy, and resources back into the hands of those who held power from black people. From studying the Willie Lynch document and other slave masters writings on the same topic, I noticed that the system of slavery was successful based on control, therefore creating divisions mainly between the male & female of the black race. Class, education, material acquisition, age, and shade are all illusions within the illusion forged by the Euro-gentile system of mind control.

For this purpose "Breaking The Curse Of Willie Lynch" was written to explain in detail the psychology behind the idea of this conditioning process, and prove that 85% of the black population are unconsciously unaware that their actions are still rooted in yesterday's slavery. Secondly my attempt was to stress the importance of the mental history that black people have as well as our biological accomplishments, and to distinguish between the two. One is the recognition of intuitive memory, which in African spirituality, is called "ancestry".

My intention was to share with you, in depth, the level of detrimental attachment to an economic system that for obvious reasons is on its way out, and help to stimulate the black consciousness to a state of overall cooperation in order that we may liberate ourselves from 446 years of spiritual violence; and then free ourselves in an economic manner. A base in strong economics will only become a reality once black people are able to boast of a healthy family unit.

Bibliography

1. The Suppression of the African Slave Trade
to the United States of America 1638-1870
W.E.B. DuBois

2. The Western Slave Coast and It's Rulers
Newburry

3. The African Slave Trade, Pre Colonial History
Basil Davidson

4. Dirty Little Secrets by Claud Anderson

5. KINLOCH Missouri's First Black City
John A. Wright Sr.

6. WITHOUT SANCTUARY
Lynching Photography in America
Twin Palms Publishers

To order your copy, please send this order form to!

RSP **Rising Sun Publications**

11220 W. Florissant Ave. # 206 · Florissant, MO 63033

1-866-899-0822

Please Send:

_____Copies of "Breaking The Curse Of Willie Lynch"

Send Money Order for $ 9.95
Plus $ 3.00 shipping & handling to:

_____ Copies of "Killing In The Name Of Love"
Genocide Of A Nation

Send Money Order for $13.95
Plus $ 3.00 Shipping & handling to:

Name_____

Address_____

City:_____State:_____Zip:_____

Charge by Visa / Master Card # _____

Exp.Date_____ Interbank #_____

Signature_____

www.risingsunpublications.com

To order your copy, please send this order form to!

RSP **Rising Sun Publications**
11220 W. Florissant Ave. # 206 · Florissant, MO 63033

1-866-899-0822
Please Send:
_____Copies of "Breaking The Curse Of Willie Lynch"

Send Money Order for $ 9.95
Plus $ 3.00 shipping & handling to:

_____ Copies of "Killing In The Name Of Love"
Genocide Of A Nation

Send Money Order for $13.95
Plus $ 3.00 Shipping & handling to:

Name_____

Address_____

City:_____State:_____Zip:_____

Charge by Visa / Master Card # _____

Exp.Date_____ Interbank #_____

Signature_____

www.risingsunpublications.com